A CONCISE GU

GW01086584

A

BAROMETER

Including Reading & Calibrating,

Predicting the Weather,

Headaches, Moods,

Hunting, Fishing

&

Other Practical Information about Barometers

by

Nathan Newton

ISBN: 979-8-7646-8429-1

CONTENTS

Chapter   **Page**

Introduction 4

Calibration and Reading 5

The Science of Barometric Pressure 10

Weather Forecasting 15

Headaches 20

Joint Pain 24

Mood 27

Low Barometric Pressure Fatigue 30

Fishing & Hunting 32

History 35

*F*or many, the barometer is a bit of a mystery. Yes, most of us know it measures air pressure, but what does that mean? How does a person use barometric pressure to predict the weather? Can pressure really affect your health, mood, or any number of other things? Even if it does, how will a barometer help? Well, let's find out. First of all, let's start with setting up your barometer so you can get the most out of it.

CALIBRATION AND READING

The first thing with you need to do with any barometer is to calibrate or set it. This is the process of adjusting it to the correct setting for your location and elevation. To do this you need to find the official barometric pressure closest to your area. (The terms barometric pressure, atmospheric pressure, or just pressure, simply refer to the measurement of air pressure exerted at a given point on Earth.)

One easy way to establish your local barometric pressure is to go to **weather.gov** (weather.com also works but has a lot of advertising) and put in your zip code. Hit enter and it will bring up the weather for your area, and a host of other things, but you want to look for the number after the words barometer or pressure. If the station or airport it is using to give you the barometric pressure is within 50 miles it should be reasonably correct.

The pressure value most used is sea level pressure, since pressure changes with altitude. This removes the effects of elevation from the pressure reading. In other words, it is the pressure that would exist at sea level at a point directly below the station.

The barometric pressure number will be shown as "in", which is short for inches, or "mb" short for millibars. These are the units of measure on the

Note: Unless you have a very expensive barometer, you may find that even after you adjust your barometer, it may not always read exactly the same as your local station. However, for most of us, this is not a problem since your focus will be the direction, speed and distance of pressure change, and not so much on the actual reading.

barometer dial. The unit most commonly used in the USA is inches and will show on your barometer dial with the numbers generally ranging from around 28  to 31 inches. Or in millibars (mb), with a range of about 950 to 1050 mb. Or your dial may have both measurements. When using inches, you will be reading in hundredths of an inch, for example, 29.23 inches which is equal to 990 mb.

Next, you will see a small screw on the back of your barometer. Usually, this is a screw that is recessed below the back surface. Turn it slowly with a screwdriver till the longer needle matches the current pressure reading you got from your local weather report.

The second needle is called a marker needle

that is used to keep track of changes. You can adjust it from the front using the knob in the middle of the glass. When taking readings, lightly tap the glass on the front to get a more accurate reading as this can free any mechanical sticking in the internal linkage of your barometer.

---

*You will find there are many different and confusing units of measurement for air pressure. Here are some of the ones appearing on barometers. Inches of mercury or **inHg**, or just **inches,** is most used in the US. The **mb** or millibar is widely used and is exactly equal to the hectopascal or **hPa**. Kilopascal or **kPa** and millimeters of mercury or **mmHg** are sometimes also used on barometer dials*

It should be noted that barometers normally do not make very large or sudden moves (unless you're in the middle of a hurricane!), so it is important to closely look at the scale on the dial so as to get a correct reading and see small changes. This brings up the fact that along with knowing how to read a barometer you will also need patience.

Tracking small changes is when that shorter marker needle (usually gold in color) becomes useful. If you look at your barometer in the morning you can line up the shorter marker needle on top of the longer needle. Then later in the day when you check it again, you can see what changes have occurred. Using that information, you can make tomorrow's weather prediction. So that's it, your barometer is adjusted, and you now know how to read it. But let's talk a little about the science behind air pressure so you can understand how barometric pressure works.

THE SCIENCE OF BAROMETRIC PRESSURE

Before we can understand what a barometer can do, we need to understand a little of the science behind barometric pressure. Barometric pressure or atmospheric air pressure is simply the weight of the air above you pushing down. Of course, it's not just pushing down, but since we are immersed in air it is really pushing in on us from all sides. To visualize how air pressure works, think of diving into a pool. The deeper you go the more pressure you feel on your eardrums. In fact, it can quickly become very painful the deeper you go. Air is very similar, but being less dense, the effects are more gradual.

We don't feel it, but we have about 14.7 lbs pushing in on us at sea level. This is an average pressure that will become less as you move higher and of course, more as you go lower.

Altitude

As an example, if you drive up a steep road the air pressure decreases and you get the sensation of your ears popping. This is because the pressure in your ears is not equal to the pressure around you.

The popping sensation is your body equalizing itself to the lower pressure. The pressure that is causing that popping, is the same pressure your barometer is measuring.

Weather

So what causes atmospheric pressure to constantly change in one area?

The short answer is the sun. With the earth constantly spinning around the Sun, different parts of the earth are being heated by day and cooled by night. Clouds drop rain or snow while at the same time reflecting the sun away from the ground, and wind moves the air around and numerous other factors create chaos in the atmosphere.

Everything in the atmosphere is in a constant state of movement and change which is why atmospheric pressure is always changing.

Temperature and Wind

When air cools, it falls, which in turn creates high pressure near the ground. The opposite happens when the air warms and rises to create regions of low pressure near the ground. So very simply: higher temperature creates higher pressure, and colder temperature creates lower pressure.

How this works is that warm temperature air is less dense, therefore lighter, and so it rises. Think of a hot air balloon. When you heat the air inside the balloon, the balloon rises because the heated air is less dense than the colder air around it, so the balloon floats up into the sky. On the other hand, cold air is denser, weighs more, and so it sinks.

The effect is that as the warm air rises, cooler air will often move in to replace it which causes wind. The greater the difference between high and low pressure, or the shorter the distance between high and low-pressure areas, the faster the wind will blow.

What is a Bomb Cyclone?
This is simply a storm that intensifies very quickly. They form when air near Earth's surface rises quickly, triggering a sudden drop in barometric pressure. To be called a bomb, it needs to drop at least .70 inches or 24 mb within 24 hours.

Technically it is not called a hurricane, but it can look and act similarly.

Humidity

Humidity goes opposite to what you would think. While it would seem, humid air would be heavier, water vapor is actually less dense and therefore lighter than dry air. So if you had two containers with one containing humid air and the other dry air, and if both were the exact same temperature, the container with the humid air would be the lightest. Therefore, if humidity increases, pressure generally decreases.

Now that you have a brief understanding of atmospheric pressure, lets now see how pressure can be used to predict the weather.

WEATHER FORECASTING

Most barometers have the words **Stormy, Rain, Change, Fair, Very Dry** around the top half of the barometer. These labels have been on barometers since the mid-1800's. Unfortunately, if the arrow is pointing at them it does not necessarily mean that will be the next day's forecast.

However, the labels do have some value. For example, when the needle is on "**Stormy**" (or below 29 inches or 980 mb) you can be sure it will be bad weather. Also, when  the needle is on "**Very Dry**" (or above 30.4 inches or 1030 mb) you can be sure it will indeed be very dry and sunny.

The rest of the dial labels may not apply depending on how the pressure is moving. This is where a basic principle comes into play. *It is not the actual barometric pressure that is important in forecasting weather, it is the direction, distance, and rate of change in pressure that determines a forecast.*

For example, as a general rule, if the pressure is quickly falling, the weather will get worse. On the other hand, if it is quickly rising it will get better, no matter where on the dial the movement starts. However, if the move is small there may be little or no change in the weather. But the bigger and faster the move the more dramatic the change in weather. This is not always the case, but on the average it is more likely.

Generally, barometers can predict the weather over the coming 12–24 hours or so. Some weather conditions can stall for days and weeks, in which case it will be that long before you may see any substantial difference on your barometer.

But, if the pressure on your barometer is steadily falling at .15 inches or 5 mb in a 6 hour period, it is a very good chance bad weather is on its way. And on the flip side, if your

The Guinness Book of Records reports that the highest air pressure ever recorded was 1084 mb (32 inches) at Agata Siberia in December 1968. The lowest was 870 mb (25.69 inches) in a typhoon in Guam in 1979 that had wind speeds of 190 mph.

barometer is steadily rising at the same rate you likely will have good weather coming your way.

As you can see, what may appear to be small changes on the barometer dial, can make a big difference. It really boils down to taking the time to regularly watch your barometer with the principles we just reviewed in mind. If you do, you will find yourself being able to predict the weather based on your barometer readings.

Of course, keeping track of changes can be tedious and easily forgotten if you are not always paying attention. If you have a smartphone you might find it helpful to supplement your regular barometer on the wall with a barometer app. Some are better than others but you should get one that gives you alerts that you can set yourself for a change in pressure.

One last point about the dial. Even though "**Change**" is at the top center of the dial, on average, your barometer will spend most of its time off to the right hovering over Fair. At least that is the case for most locations.

So, there you have it, now you can start predicting the weather with your barometer, it's that easy! But let's talk about some other practical ways you can use your barometer.

HEADACHES

With many headache sufferers, this is a big area of interest, and for good reason. Scientific studies have revealed that there indeed is a connection between barometric pressure and headaches or migraines.

The way it is understood is that our sinuses, which are filled with air, push out against the normal air pressure around you to maintain a balance. But when the atmospheric air pressure

Headaches vs Migraine

Headaches *can range from mild to severe pain, but usually gives pain on both sides of your head, and feels like pressure rather than throbbing. Other symptoms may be soreness in your temples, neck, and shoulders.*

Migraines *are caused by imbalances in brain chemistry. Pain can range from moderate to severe throbbing pain that may be worse on one side of your head, eyes, or temple, with sensitivity to light, sounds, and smells. May also include nausea, and see wavy lines, dots, or flashing lights. The pain gets worse with physical activity.*

drops the pressure in the sinuses is now greater than the outside pressure and this, in turn, seems to trigger headaches. On top of that if you have congestion, allergies, or sinus issues the problem can be worse.

Oddly enough you would normally think high barometric pressure would press in on your head and be the cause of pain, however, high barometric pressure seems to actually relieve headaches in most people.

Recall that low pressure is often associated with bad weather. So, if you notice your headaches often happen during bad weather you might want to check your barometer to see if there is a connection between pressure dropping and your headaches.

One study discovered migraine frequency increased on days when the pressure lowered by just over .15 inches (5 mb) from the previous day. But the migraines correspondingly decreased when the pressure went back up by the same amount. A similar study found that migraines occurred most frequently when the atmospheric pressure decreased by .15 - .3 inches (6-10 mb).

As you can see from these studies the pressure drop does not have to be that much, for people dealing with chronic headaches or migraines.

Another large-scale study found that sales of Loxoprofen were mostly purchased for headaches and that these sales increased when the barometric pressure decreased.

In any event, you can't change the weather, but if you are a headache sufferer, understanding barometric pressure's effect on your headaches can be a huge help. This is why it is important for you to closely watch your barometer and notice what amount of changes in pressure affect your specific headaches.

Once you understand what pressure changes trigger your specific headaches, you can now be forewarned. With that piece of information, you will be confident that any small sign you feel of a headache coming on is *real,* and begin treating yourself early before it gets ahold of you. As any headache sufferer knows, early treatment often is the difference between a relatively small headache and a debilitating one.

JOINT PAIN

Remember when grandpa would say there is a storm coming because his knee started to hurt? The reality is that he may have been correct. In fact, for many people, there is definitely a connection between barometric pressure, body pain, and stiffness.

One thing to keep in mind is that body

aches associated with the weather may be different from one person to the next. In addition to arthritis, joint pain, and stiffness, others report pain from scar tissue, tendons, and muscle pain.

While doctors and researchers are not exactly sure why barometric pressure changes cause pain, there are a few theories that seem to make sense.

It is often noted that a drop in barometric pressure leads to increased swelling in the joints which in turn leads to pain. The thought is that as pressure drops there is less pressure to push against the body. This allows tissues around the joints to expand, putting pressure on the joints and increasing pain.

Another idea is that when the cartilage that cushions the bones inside a joint is worn away, nerves in the exposed bones more readily pick up on changes in pressure, which leads to pain.

One last idea is that low pressure accompanied with cooler temperature from bad weather causes the contraction of scar tissue, ligaments, tendons, and cartilage within the joint and this is what causes the increase in pain.

Unfortunately, your barometer may only be able to confirm what you already know. But look on the bright side, and just think, if this is how pressure affects you, now you can combine it with your barometer readings to predict the weather and impress your friends!

MOOD

Have you been getting a little moody lately? Well, guess what, it may be that you are being affected by low atmospheric air pressure!

A study conducted at Olin Neuropsychiatry Research Center in Connecticut compared more than 3,000 MRI scans with hourly weather reports and discovered an association between barometric pressure and brain size. When the barometric pressure drops, the cerebellum (a small part of the brain located at the back) shrinks but the rest of the brain grows in size.

The study did not reach any specific conclusion, however, a number of other studies have connected low pressure with increased acts of negative behavior.

In Japan, a rather strange study was done using rats. The rats were forced to swim to the point of becoming immobile. Later they were given antidepressants and found the rats swam longer indicating that the immobility was anxiety/depression like behavior.

The experiment was repeated without antidepressants, but instead using a climate-controlled room. They compared the effects of normal barometric pressure with a lower pressure of .6 inches (20 mb). When the rats were forced to swim under natural atmospheric pressure, they did so for significantly longer than when under lower pressure. The conclusion was that low barometric pressure seemingly made the poor rats depressed to the point they stopped swimming!

On the more human side of things, other

studies have shown a correlation between low barometric pressure and an increase in impulsive and aggressive behaviors. It was observed that there was a sizable increase in the number of acts of violence and emergency psychiatry visits when the barometric pressure lowered.

So for the most part high pressure seems to put people is a good mood. Some even suggest using a barometer to determine when to do business or ask someone a favor! But no one seems to have a good idea as to why barometric pressure appears to have this effect. But as you are probably noticing by now, low atmospheric air pressure doesn't seem to sit too well with us humans for any number of reasons. Whether directly or indirectly a host of things associated with low pressure can add up to putting us in a bad mood. So go ahead and blame it on barometric pressure!

LOW BAROMETRIC PRESSURE
FATIGUE

Do rainy days make you tired? Well, there is actually a phrase for that, "low barometric pressure fatigue". That's right, low pressure can also make you tired.

Low pressure is understood to increase the thickness of your blood especially when accompanied by lower temperatures, which makes it harder to control blood sugar levels. When you have low blood sugar fatigue sets in.

Low atmospheric pressure accompanied by cooler temperatures also causes your blood vessels to constrict. This in turn will cause your blood pressure to increase because it takes more pressure to move blood through a narrower space. High blood pressure is another cause for feeling fatigued and tired.

It is also felt by some that lower atmospheric pressure equals less oxygen in the air. While there is not much scientific data on the subject the idea is that this results in drowsiness. For example, hypoxia (a condition when the body is deprived of adequate oxygen) can cause tiredness because you aren't getting enough oxygen to stay alert.

Finally, low atmospheric pressure often occurs in conjunction with periods of lowered natural light, which sends a signal to the body to produce more melatonin. All of these factors surround our subject of atmospheric pressure and the effect it can have on feelings of tiredness.

FISHING & HUNTING

There are numerous convincing articles on the internet about why a barometer is the best way to determine when to go fishing or hunting. In fact, when it comes to fishing there are barometers designed just for that purpose. However, if you shop around for these barometers you may also notice conflicting dials. For example, some fish barometer dials show 29–29.5 inches as good fishing and others show the same measurement as poor fishing.

By way of interest, it is a fact that water is about 800 times denser than air. So, you can imagine that a fish just changing its depth by a few inches would experience a far greater change than the more gradual hourly changes in atmospheric pressure.

All is not lost, however, as a barometer certainly can be your most useful tool to predict the upcoming weather that will affect cloud cover, precipitation, air, and correspondingly water temperature. All of which will have an effect on the fish, and fisherman!

As far as barometric pressure affecting the movements of land animals this is certainly a reasonable factor. Different species are affected directly. For example, birds tend to fly lower when the pressure is low, to take advantage of the denser air. This is also why low flying birds can be a sign of poor weather on the way.

Land animals like humans are also affected. Many reported unusual behaviors of animals before a storm indicates animals' sensitivity to approaching storms. Since we can't interview them we do not know what animals are actually sensing but we definitely see the effects on them. One hunter after years of observations noted greater deer activity at high pressure especially when the barometer passes 30 inches.

So, depending on the species, the observations of humans can sometimes connect high or low pressure to specific animal behavior. So, this can be a great indicator but it is very much contingent on the specific animal and how it reacts to the change in pressure.

It all started in 1643, when Evangelista Torricelli was trying to figure out how high water could be pumped, and discovered 33 feet was the limit at which no matter how hard they tried they could pump no higher. In trying to figure things out they made an experiment that consisted of filling a long tube with water and then plugging both ends. They then stood the

tube up in a basin full of water. The bottom end of the tube was opened, and water that had been inside of it poured out into the basin. However,

only part of the water in the tube flowed out, and the level of the water inside the tube stayed at that same level of 33 feet.

Torricelli reasoned that it must be the weight of the air pushing down on the water in the basin at the base that was forcing the water up the tube. In other words, without any air pressing down on the tube of water the weight of the air pressing down on the water at the base was equal to the weight of the water in the tube.

This was a new idea since most at that time believed that air had no weight. About then Torricelli's neighbors got to talking about this contraption of his and decided he must be into some form of sorcery or witchcraft! Torricelli realized he had to keep his experiment secret to avoid the risk of being arrested. So, he switched the liquid over to mercury which is about 14 times heavier than water. The result was that the 33 foot column of water was now just 29 inches.

Over the next few decades, the instrument was further studied and developed to understand how it could also predict weather and measure altitude. The interesting thing is that to this day we are still using inches of mercury to get barometric pressure readings.

While the mercury barometer was useful it was not very easy to move or carry around. But in 1844 Lucien Vidie designed, built, 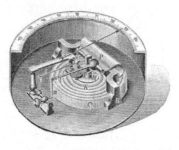 and patented the first successful Aneroid barometer. Aneroid means without liquid, and instead of mercury, it uses a vacuum sealed metal bellow that expands and contracts in response to the atmospheric pressure. A clock style mechanism then transfers the expansion and contraction to a dial that shows the pressure, which is how your barometer works.

In recent years there has been the development and switch to electronic barometers. They also show up on smartphones and watches which if you have a smartphone, you can access by downloading a barometer app. However, don't be fooled that they are necessarily more accurate! Interestingly the inner working of the sensor used to give you a digital reading are basically a microscopic mechanical barometer. A small membrane flexes in or out according to the pressure, and then an electronic sensor reads the change and sends it to a digital display.

Something to keep in mind if you are using your smartphone or watch for barometric readings is that if you see sudden jumps in pressure it does not necessarily mean your device is wrong. It may simply be that you were traveling and you indeed quickly drove into and out of a pressure system, or more likely, you changed altitude and this is what created the sudden change.

So now you can say you are barometer smart. Start putting it into practice and you will be barometer wise. But don't get too carried away, a wise proverb in the bible says, *"The one who watches the wind will not sow seed, and the one who looks at the clouds will not reap."* ***Ecclesiastes 11:4***

References

Influence of Barometric Pressure in Patients with Migraine Headache
https://www.jstage.jst.go.jp/article/internalmedicine/50/18/50_18_1923/_pdf

Examination of fluctuations in atmospheric pressure related to migraine
https://www.ncbi.nlm.nih.gov/pmc/articles/PMC4684554/

Weather and headache onset: a large-scale study of headache medicine purchases
https://link.springer.com/article/10.1007%2Fs00484-014-0859-8

Weather Changes Brain Size, Affecting Physical, Psychiatric Conditions
https://healthnewshub.org/new-research-weather-changes-brain-size-affecting-physical-psychiatric-conditions/

Lowering barometric pressure aggravates depression-like behavior in rats
https://www.sciencedirect.com/science/article/abs/pii/S0166432810007825

Barometric Pressure, Emergency Psychiatric Visits, and Violent Acts
https://pubmed.ncbi.nlm.nih.gov/14631883/

Weather and Aggressive Behavior among Patients in Psychiatric Hospitals-An Exploratory Study
https://pubmed.ncbi.nlm.nih.gov/33297298/

Printed in Great Britain
by Amazon